Tenants on this
PLANET

F R A N K   K A R A N

Copyright © 2021 by Frank Karan.

ISBN- 978-1-6379-0121-2 (sc)
ISBN- 978-1-6379-0232-5 (hc)
ISBN- 978-1-6379-0233-2 (eBook)

All rights reserved. No part of this book may be reproduced or transmitted in any form or by any means, electronic or mechanical, including photocopying, recording, or by any information storage and retrieval system, without permission in writing from the copyright owner.

The views expressed in this work are solely those of the author and do not necessarily reflect the views of the publisher, and the publisher hereby disclaims any responsibility for them.

Matchstick Literary
1-888-306-8885
orders@matchliterary.com

AESTHETICALLY DRAINED

Your still reading scripts an reciting sonnets
Written by crafty writers and frustrated poets
Your body feels ritually aesthetically drained
And you're mind meanders enchantingly strained

Yet you still maintain yourself so gorgeously cute
Even when you childishly play the shepherd's flute
Your happy soul cries briskly like the avenging wind
Leaving me with little nothing but to cheerfully sin

While ludicrously babbling in various forms of acerbic tongue
Basking in a forsaken glitchy world filled with irregular fun
Aspiratedly seeking out the most ennoble existentialist ideals
Which disturbingly prove to be pragmatic an frighteningly real

ANGUISHED PAUSES

You're cautiously observing events from a safe distance
Supposedly there is no resistance only anguished pauses
Taking that admirably expunged, time honoured patient stance
Confidently displaying the utterly lamentable oneshot chance

Juxtapositionally arranged in a sequentially lapsing trance
It's akin to burning hundred dollar notes, without a glance
Such originally diverge complicit is miscreantly subserved
Gussying up to you're tameable dog eared friend unperturbed

Randomnessly pumping out it's semi quaver saddened song
Faintly but surely harmonising in a syncopated madrigal
Exposing the miscalculated, unmeritoriously eccentric claims
Your methodology is somewhat questionable, lacking any gains

AWKWARD REVISION

How will you allocate your resources
When confronted by a near impossible
No win situation? Which tactics, shall you
Employ to limit the risk of sudden failure

You're unskilled pithy methods of diagnosis
Lack substantial refinement, so you need to
Readjust your mindset into more solid decision
The unfinished categories need sharp precision

What considerable suspicions have been quoted and
Divulged by the proper authorities? Rescinding in
Such improptu repertoire of fierce quarrelsome indecision
Can some positive things arise from this awkward revision

BARREN SOUL

You need some time out, to bury the bloody rotting dead
Then you can extricately examine your old battered head
There's no momentous occasion; only a destabilising abrasion
Your analytical mind is fobbling inside the goldy conflation

Where's the die hard substitute embedded in your imagination?
Vainly searching the gobsmacked emptiness of your barren soul
Luxuriously riding in a turquoise scented horsedrawn carriage
In an unknown destination; obscurely procreating by summation

BELATED AGONY

You're a weary bloodied soldier
Coming back from the bloody war
Rumbling between pain n'mumbling
Tales of gore; smirking abruptly

With your sullen, ahoehorned face
Your besotted soul lies tarnished
In undulating misery, there's only
Grief, to subdue the belated agony

The simple rest that you seek
Is reserved only for the meek
Yet you crave for something deep
Maybe you can see it. In your sleep

BENEVOLENT INDISCRETION

With caringly observant fatherly interests, you
Keep tracklisting the brushstrokes of obscurity
Which are otherwise invisible for anyone to see
Downloading those engaging performances of life

The loveliness you show is undeniably bewildering
Like an intrepid explorer accidentally uncovering
An antique plaque, on some mythical ancient site
Hummed in with festering benevolent indiscretion

The twinkle in your eye exhibits simmering repression
As you're blushness, highlights real inducing passion
This inevitable dilemma has artificially inseminated
It's cul de sac sour flavouring meandering obsession

BLEEDING HEART

In another blissful time an place
I trace the emotions, which I can
Feel no more; a cobblestone broke
The surface of the shiny silent lake
That made the fish scared then awake

Bringing ripples of lonely tears to my
Pithy hurting bleeding heart once more
Then I learned from your surprising disguise
Were we not comfortably meant to be together
In a romantic liaison, with a bottle of wine

BLINDING DESIRE

Your mind is compounded by ceaseless banging shutters
Which retain you from having a peaceful night's sleep
You're life is akin to a blinding desire that's yet to be
Fulfilled like searching for oil that needs to be drilled

That's why you fly yourself like a lazy bird
In the sky, soaring above the marksman's eye
As you recklessly try jockeying to be the first
But your always irritatingly denying your worth

You exude yourself so precociously alert, as you
Extensively surround nobly, with renaissance art
Constantly thumbling wildly with a fiendish part
Ameliorating your rank, without any sneaky prank

There's a goady blowing breeze; as we ride over
The winding hills listening to earful slapdowns
Ambit claims of historically fossilized remains
There is knowledge that has yet to be exchanged

MEMORIES CAPSULED

When the moon shines brightly thru the dusk clouds
Moving the waves, in shades of blue across the sea
My heart will gently receive your love as it flows
Into me; you're locked in the prison without a key

Trying to be free! Anointing yourself with precious
Gifts; capsuled memories shall awaken on your shift
Whilst swimming in the ocean, with anxious caring hands
Rolling on a beach of xanthic crystallized golden sands

The distillation of uniting tears hides the facade
From the chequerboard for pent up unsociable fears
Rising up to the sun's early rays, I somehow wonder
If we shall experience thundery, showery humid days

Sleeping on the park bench, haggling in dire stench
There's a warm breeze soothingly blowing in my back
Shaking off the venomous slack! So why do you consume
Sour apples in the morning? When you're still yawning

CONFIDENTLY COMMUNICATE

I am audaciously searching for answers, in my endeavours
But I'm constantly faced with a confusing array of ideas
With my deep widening knowledge I try to understand the
Various thoughts of wise men; their riddles and enigmas

There are many unfolding stories n'competing world views
Highlighted by the elite few! As a naive observer I must
Confidently communicate our honourable intentions with a
Commanding stance, resurrecting an incorruptible romance

CONFISCATED MOBILITY

Abruptly your reorganizing yourself expediatingly fast
Explicably contradicting the double meanings, expelled
By your sadistically barbarous psyche; then you step into
The same old circus with a zealously demanding ringmaster

Languidly shunning n'repeating obscenities variably interwoven
An so impeccably timed. All the dastardly deeds shall be mined
Dripping with dismissive patriotism and besmirching solid reputations
Penned into mythology are the silliest mediocre cumbersome situations

Transported by large electric trains carrying the heaviest of freight
Whilst running off the unforseeable track, to a self exhausting whack
From such a brief astute campaign of autonomously void compossibility
Lacking agility an formidably crystallizing into confiscated mobility.

CONIFEROUS BREEZE

The memories of you I will always save
My heart was glued to you so I forgave
We did reach tallish unscalable heights
Though we had so many unpleasant fights

We're listening to tiny windchat birds
Singing in the lofty coniferous breeze
The furry squirrels easily run up the trees
How I miss n'cherish my cheeky little tease

The enchanting voices of the alluring sirens
Keep whingeing into the distant starry night
My muscles are begging to rest n'shaking in fright
I'm unnervingly overwhelmed by this horrible sight

CYCLICAL VOLATILITY

Blindingly you sink into the refreshing bubbly bath
Trying to unify a much beleaguered pervasive system
Which exhibits a vast array of plausible resistance
Charting the credible path to a profitable recovery
Just by digging deeper you make a notable discovery

Which simultaneously heralds the previous archaeological find
Cost cutting your measely expenditure with a sundry allowance
You show the upmost diligent resillience, from peak to trough
Carefully screening the unforeseen consequences n'cyclical volatility
Are you're instruments usually blunt? When you pursue the savage hunt

DECEPTIVELY TRANSIENT

Strolling past layers of mountain sand
The sunflinged salty hot waters reveal
The unnatural coral bleaching of the reef
The deceptively transient drainage system

Is continually drifting offshore; the tall rocky cliffs
Are embelished with Triassic fossils which still remain
The shadding boulders are submerged with myths from the
Golden era of classical domain, like a sage without age

There's not even a single shaky green leaf, to offer some
Cooling relief in this dried up flowerless bathless barge
Unbeknowingly to our senses this mirage carries little despair
Our lives are hankered with complexity trying to get somewhere

DELEVERAGING SCENARIO

Fat bubbles are dancing cheerily in your teacup
Indicating the caffeination level is resonantly
Narcistically sleepy faced and so tenderly warm
Robust winds keep blowing seasaly deleteriously

Onto the island grass as the volcanic ash seeps
It's way into the once pristine browny red soil
Prudently avoiding the glut from poorly managed
Farms which have been squeezed out of existence

Your deleveraging scenario is cheekily designed
Uptiding those commendable strategies employing
Drastic overhauls constantly removing obstacles
Whilst trialling all recent avant garde methods

We texturally perform a perfectly new balancing act
In order to keep what we have, and to less subtract
Unleashing untapped reserves; strangling the parrot
Can you extract enough fresh juice? From the carrot

DUTY OF SERENITY

There's so many ghost stories which you can write about
With pathetically conflating, sorry ill mannered humour
You're so mysteriously vague, sitting sullen an so dimply depraved
Are you sure your not intravenously concocted or artificially made

Your lips taste like burnt raw sugar with a splash of mint
Why are you so stubborn? That you can't take a subtle hint
You've been flexibly commandeered travelling on a highjacked plane
Turning off all those transponders, to avoid any form of detection

Must you scoff at all of the contorting antagonistic rejection
Our duty of serenity aptly renegotiates any probable ascension
As we exclusively tiptoe to avoid smattering the detailed attention
Kinetically smothering the rambunctious fame with a soft transition

You're opportunistic fractious self is locked up in your twisted psyche
Research an experimentation advances our understanding n'reductive clar
Is there any hidden inherent weakness in your carefully laid out plan
Is there some strategy to enhance you're highly skilled military span

ECLECTIC HATE

There's a unanimous inflexion of uninterrupted love
As I yearn for your sugary lips, n'frosty damp kiss
Splattering into my vodka dry chilled soaking mouth
Your exfoliating smile and vile gutturally displays

It's snowdowned soggy, cold wintery lapse
The slightest fluttering seduces the apse
Incompatability is an interfering rebuttal
Venturing into, the orbiting space shuttle

Acknowledging the unprepared mechanism of eclectic hate
Swiftly we gather round the table, before the next date
Substituting an integral variety of emotions on a plate
The universal condition for forgiveness, is served late

ENCHANTING CAVE

I feel like I've been asleep for at
Least a thousand frustrating years!
But now I have awoken without any worrying fears
I am silently shedding the nasty heartfelt tears

Plucking the melodious strings of ecstasy
MY spiritual tail quails an gently exhales
I'm rigorously exhuming the long lost dusty
Desert cowboy trail for me to fiercely avail

I'm feeling somewhat less than brave, as I enter
The mouth of the flinty slippery enchanting cave
The texture of the night has inconsolably strained
As I hurtle myself and shakingly pivot so deranged

There's something peculiar in the interstellar rhyme
Where the flickering sun, just doesn't seem to shine
Or to sink dully down, into the devouring dark blue sea
I can still rejoice; because I know that you're with me

ESCAPE TO SCREAM

A freshly baked souffle rises only once
But my love for you constantly crops up
Why are you sipping soup? At that old
Fashioned rundown bohemian restaurant

Wouldn't you prefer to be drinking coffee
At a brand new cosy upmarket, trendy cafe
There' an anthill of progressive workers
Busily passing by, waiting for a break in

Order to excel and fly! What advantages do
They possess and why? Can they really try?
There some unexpected relief from the
Tediously dull comments that whisper by

Whirlingly you vie to catch my happy vibe
As you drowsily wave back and forth at me
Panting wildly, you frantically escape to scream
Floating gently in the sky in a comforting dream

EXISTENTIALIST EXPENSE

The sweetness of your soft honeysuckle kiss
Has lathered my tongue with frivolous bliss
My grieving head lays nestling on your breast
As the mid afternoon sun gently intrudes over

The woodfire oven's freshly baked aroma bread
The greyishly darkening day is tugged between
Sheets of mangy red skies; reimagining blushing
Cloudy sour eyes! What a minute dismal surprise

Do you believe in some divine intervention or any
Cosmic intention? Is there tangible proof of such
Conspiracy or a counter intuitive nominalistic fluency
This confirmational vibe is conceptually shrouded with

A spatio temporal abstract platonism, deplorably
Interpreting the perceptual defence; at your own
Existentialist expense! You may have to take off
Your creasy sweaty shirt, to enjoy an easy flirt

EXTRACURRICULAR AIMS

Your vile sentiments are so breathtakingly furious
Yet intuitively precise and contentiously proposed
I'm commenting coyly on the aggregate assumptions
That require gut wrenching but nervy presumptions

A rapid adjustment has submerged your frying brains
We all need to restore some dignity after exploring
These demeaning games; overstretching frenzied gains
We're contumaciously toiling in extracurricular aims

Grappling in the amassed worldwide geographic network
While obstinately accomodating various neutral plains
Sanctimoniously severed with overabundant hellish flames
Further fertilising the mutually reciprocal messed pains

By pocketing proceeds imperial titles misallocate claims
Which priest has never consoled the adulterer
What unexpected benefits shall the meek crave
When they're only an expendable pitiful slave

FAINT SYLLABLE

You're life is like watching a satirical popcorn comedy movie
Shot in 35 millimetre black an white poor quality grainy film
Presumably you've glimpsed, at lifeless cardboard characters
Enhanced by flicking on the revolving shutter speed aperture

There are many treasured memories, to recollect and reconnect
Drabbily you dress like some old fashioned Antarctic explorer
Perhaps you'd want to show us that your earnestly much poorer
Today I visited my aging sick father in the private hospital

As I shaved his husky white growing beard, I attentively held
His dull face in my clean wet cold hands and I wiped away the
Sweat from his eyebrows then I acknowledged how he held me
Some fifty years earlier, passionately I eagerly held onto

Every faint syllable his heavily grunting voice had spoken
I never thought I'd feel this way towards him, he reminded
Me of a little lost lamb so frail n'pale, finally I conceded that the
Day had come, to leave all off the bitchy arquing and the
    damage done

FAMISHED HEART

Eagerly your trying to shatter the unsettled present
But you cannot pleasantly return to the passive past
It's so undecisive, to be labelled a tyrannical outcast
There are many milky air bubbles rising along your path

Notched up on a compressed refracting nostalgic ambient aura
Blotched in Ill thredded retrofitted clergycal drapey attire
You're pekish stomach is squeezed; repressively in a quagmire
The famished heart cascades, like a thundering wall of desire

FAR REACHING GOALS

We lost our inhibitions over a bottle of wine
And failed to keep track of the intimate time
We ran up the cliffs with our feet in the dirt
As you frantically ripped off your silky shirt

We can storm the castle without a major hassle
In a realm of unlimited possessions mired with
Ego maniac obsessions; we can unleash unlimited
Possibilities with our industrious capabilities

We can build golden bridges over rivers of old
With comfortably drivable scenic winding roads
And powerful space rockets, which will explode
Humanity desires to achieve far reaching goals

FLEXIBLE DEFIANCE

You're detached rampaging spirit and intrinsic curiosity
Keeps you moving ahead with holistic untameable ferocity
Periodically seeming lame surprisingly lifting your game
Trying to douse out the poisonous, erupting volcanic ash

Maraudingly sulking over the portals of mispent loyalties
With cursing screams, etched in procluding ghostly dreams
Elongating a fragile alliance, marked out in some uneasy
Flexible defiance; there's a strange abomination ensuing

Undefinably brewing into an unearthly creation,
dispensing In unsanitary scientific preparation. Is there a solution?
For our evolution! They'll be many trials and tribulations
Requiring immediate reunification, competing for salvation

FLOOD OF MISERY

Your treasonous plot has been tediously uncovered
With the treacherous henchmen disciples preaching
They're venomous hate, the bizzare escapades exploit
A demented hypocrisy revolving in a cul de sac state

Sadly, with a less than applicable inverterbrae ferocity
Culminating from an underlying existentialist philosophy
There's a treasure trove of original ideas, discordially
Exchanged at our shamelessly loud, unusual couch debates

Methodically fused in a mixture of incarcerated hate
But never accomplished fate, those angry mouldy eyes
Keep drenching me wet; as the flood of misery openly
Flows thru the gate. Shall we try to stem it's rate?

FORCIBLY ARTICULATING

Experimenting abundantly with the diriding agents of change
Causing further problems by entrenching complicit ramblings
Accelerating a messy nature of unvilified sentimental rifts
Forcibly articulating and exerting seedy recompensive gifts

The ancient blood is still crying up from our ancestral land
There's a slimy integration of pillage, at every elusive hand
From the lowest possible margins of society, we'll make a stand
Easily sliding into tragedy, will your cravings totally command

FRAUDULENTLY AFFLICTED

There's an unburdening relief brewing with contentment
Your fraudulently afflicted; by exculpatory resentment
A peripheral spectrum lies conjoined in a venality of
A souring trenchantly unwelcoming sadness; the whisky

Swigging bandits belie in elaborate subversive contempt
With a monstrous anger explosively geared within lament
I wholeheartedly deplore you're ironic admonitional consent
Your like a farmer selling his paddock to buy a new tractor

The sadder parts of childhood are like a nuclear reactor
Pseudonymous authors; are inflicted with aortic stenosis
Even when we read a coherently narrative, medical prognosis
Every life has a current! So why keep rowing into psychosis

HEARTRENDENINGLY DEFACED

There's an austere instability when it's formidably cold
Typically hatching a shell, with a torturous sampling of
Demonstrably perpetuating a bleak mind numbing structure
Buildings in distant dunes, are on the verge of collapse

The nature of neglect leaves the repository with a muddy bill
Surprisingly buried with a hostile chill and terrifying drill
The ravages of war 'pillage have left you weary 'paper thin
Plundering archaeological artefacts an murals up to your chin

The monuments that you did once worship have been
Heartrenderingly defaced! They've been abrasively
Vandalized, without any pity or justifiable grace
How thoughtlessly reckless befitting not our race

HIDDEN WHISPERS

Can you hear the hidden whispers in the trees
And the calming monotony of the autumn breeze
My heart keeps ratcheting in the open crossfire
With a subtle tease, all your worrying troubles

Lay buried beneath your stinky grubby little feet
You've learnt to beg steal and borrow with you're
Hustling teeth; rustling in the veins of your seat
The complexity of life is much more serious n'deep

HIDEOUS RASCAL

The clock keeps ticking louder by the hour
And I've been exalted, by a superior power
You're soft laughing lips teaches us new tricks
As I hungrily fumble for some tasty caviar dips

I'm tempted to lick the sugary lollies out from the jar
And exclusively redecorate your luxurious expensive car
Maybe I can play some blues licks, on my vintage guitar
You never know one day you may shine bright like a star

whilst I'm tiredly sleeping next to a burnt out log
Playfully patting the cuddly docile St. Bernard dog
I've dreamt that I'm running up the magic mountain
Marauding past the wicked witch's cryptic fountain

Clumsily I'm sifting through the misty gully, rescinding
Into the man eating glen; chittering in the dragon's den
Hurriedly I search for the king's castle as to seek refuge
From the hideous rascal, avoiding the mischievous farcical

HOBBLING ACQUISITIONS

You're inky sunburnt skin is hankering to quickly explode
The infectiously raunchy, interlocutory expensive methods
Prohibit hobbling acquisitions digesting healthy nutrition
Is there any regulatory impact swiggling at torchlit skies

Can we salvage the urban domains from the systems of explosive
Demolitions? Burning throngly bright yet excessively composive
Your wounding words are like an empty can of odourless fragrance
Which is spitefully consternating upon periously misadvantageous

In the confusing angst emerges an appellation chomped by sharks
It's as if the sting has come out of the sun; pathetically done
Contorting into a diluted version of a brainless frozen faced dummy
Dim witted you bow your head like a clown licking the icypole yummy

HUMBLY BEGGING

I hear faint little children's voices
Yelling restlessly, out in the street
They're muddy legs are running wildly
Haphazardly cringing to a louder beat

Then you violently whip me with your
Studded leather belt beneath my feet
I knelt in front of you humbly begging
To be spared this dishonourable defeat

The woody rotten stairway is halfbent
And my luck has been wastefully spent
You're torture tested unproven achievements
Don't need anymore signed sealed agreements

The boatshed of ideas has become waterlogged
With painstaking anxieties an tedious fears
You require diversity and protege proprietary
To keep yourself intact 'rise above the fact

ILLICIT MINUTES

My ambitious protege is strictly a stern perfectionist at heart
whimsically walking on a tightrope whilst synchronizing his art
Quintessentially working a rotating shift developing his stylish gift
Impartially acquisitioning the immemorably scarty,
    nonconformist rift

Accompanying me, myself and I, to some exorbitant wealthy
    supply
So how can you tackle obesity without cutting the calorie intake
Are you still suffering from suicidal tendencies; or drug
    dependancies
We have to impose limits, upon the crudely percolating illicit
    minutes

IMPLODING INSURGENCY

Your mentality is unquestionably stratosherically minded!
Constantly optimising upon the multipronged opportunities
Without been meaninglessly and egotistically blinded
Indulging yourself with an imploding insurgency from

The unauthorized incendiary 'morose demeanor, propells
Nosediving into an affraying cheeky arrogant grin whilst
Held captive in a multitude of psychedelic wonders while
Trapped in a world of inane senses with arabesque fences

IMPOSING VOID

You're like a tempestous gambler desperately
Trying his luck at each table, placing betts
Hoping to win the jackpot, there are so many
Unrealistic constraints within our lifestyle

With plentiful amounts from frenzied borrowing
The rebellious following was always quarelling
You've been twice elected, but thrice rejected
You've been abdicated 'imprisoned an dejected

Whilst branching outwards trying to break the Imposing
Void. Which interlocutions will you offer to douse out
The expanding annoid? In you're mellow reminiscing heart
Exploding like a supernova on the highway to a kickstart

IMPULSIVELY ROBOTIC

We compare beauty, to ugliness
An if everything was beautiful
Then that would be the accepted norm
Delivering us from this deadly storm

You're artistic appetite and inquisitive pursuits
Keeps on hectically tailoring, your Italian suits
Impatiently scrambling so impulsively robotic
Becomes the normatively, gritty rule of thumb

Even though, you like playing dumb
Overburdened by rudeness and shame
History shall not record your name
Bereft off the inept, plebeian jaw

You snarl and deplore; at every dullish meddlesome tedious chore
Walking thru the cemetery you hope to hear the cries of the dead
But you've gravely been misled! If you think your going to die
And come back to life; brother you're in a whole lot of strife

INDISPUTABLE CIRCUMSTANCES

We're faintly skating on the edge of the slippery cliff
Embracing our lonesome love in a sultry diehard silence
Travelling on the relevveled road to a sustainable recovery
whilst strengthening the inappropriate, regulatory dynamics

Boosting the bubbling pumice priming intricate ceramics
Angrily you're seething; like the starving wolf's teeth
As you cowardly run'hide, underneath the worn out wooly sheet
which indisputable circumstances catastrophically lie beneath

INNOCENT CRIME

The lightning sparkled violently, in the winter's sky
As I gladly reminisced, about the lovely days gone by
Remnants of pledging love; silvery clouds trail above
Nature created all that's beautifully good and divine

Love keeps enveloping us in a tingling frothy mist
Matchmaking ourselves with a bright heavenly twist
My heart still pays dearly for it's innocent crime
The desire of wanting to be with you, for all time

JAGGEDLY FRAYED

Your wound is inflicted with poison
An will probably never heal, so you
Willingly use that as some valid excuse to
Hate maim n'kill! This cloak 'dagger tale

Wreaks full of turbid surprises, sinisterly you
Stealthily mock n'chill, with a ghostly thrill!
Percolating within the jittery cold minutes
From a concomitant of jaggedly frayed ego's

With the parlance of pitching crescendo
Blipping past the fettled burble n'bark
Waving madly amongst escalating fiery tempers of
The subconsciously hidden; prisoners of the dark

KNOTTY VORTEX

There's no instant attraction or warmly mild delayed
Reaction, in response to your sexual dissatisfaction
They're are many sad stories blogging around in my head
An plenty of icy crystals lagging mildly on my soft bed

My lips are sizzling very hot an red, as you're arms
Keep flapping wildly in the breezy humid air instead
Uncontrollably jeering at your long overdue ascension
Into the worthy realm of elite covert loss prevention

Your sly ex girlfriend with the ugly false teeth
Is like a leech trying to suck my delicate blood
I feel so awkward that I'd rather get washed away
In the knotty vortex of a hurricane typhoon flood

LABYRINTH OF PENSIVE

Your intensifying earthly charm remains attractively contagious
As my flippant eyes crisply pierce thru the slowburning candles
Upwards from the elaborately decorated crystallized chandeliers
Into you're implausibly controlled untouched, virgin naked body

How I crave to delicately apply jojoba oil in an intricately
Bubbly detailed form an rub it softly in your numbing curves
My gentle hands are very enthusiastically adorned to readily
Solidify your cruising incentive in the labyrinth of pensive

With some deliciously aspirated bulwark, cloisonne onclave hospice
Riding over the colourful filigreed surfaces and saintly reliquary
Fragrant trees perch in a non artificial warmth of a subtropical bath
The curious alchemist experiments to discern the elements of the bark

LAIDBACK TROPICANA

How I wish to slip through these cracks
Into the luxuriantly laidback tropicana
whilst bodysurfing on a fishnet hammock
Sipping a refreshingly cool pina colada

The rhythmic lapping of the ocean waves
Lends solitude to you're embracing gaze
Filtering in the essence of happier days
Twisting and turning into a soulful haze

I'm reluctant to return to my old ways
Even though I've been dubiously misled
You won't have to tuck me into our bed
I'll sink myself, into the bubble bath

Of freshly scented fragrant lavender oils
As I glibly read ancient texts an scrolls
Written by reclusive scholars 'mysterious mystics
Thus trying to decipher any hidden messages within

They're elusive sacred meanings and sharp puzzling words
Skimming past Newtonian physics 'assorted hieroglyphics
You're feet travelled thru revolving open an closed doors
You still voraciously crave for some thunderous applause!

But there always seems to be a sly fastening caveat clause
How far can you pierce your ferocious bloodied feline paws
Wouldn't you rather dig a hole in the sand with a giant spade
And release your angst, in the balmy laidback tropicana shade

LAMENTED SAVAGERY

You're like a curious little kid, trying to
Prove himself to the world, so when you shall
Grow up to be big wise an judgmentally strong
You'll be interrogating every morsel of stone

Wafting in the misty meadows by the mountain stream
Running thru the cloud descending haze shining like
A calm starry night, brewing in disoriented contentment
Squaring off against terrifying sword wielding bandits

Chasing them into the thin meltwatering ice; refracting
A stringency of reinforced lamented savagery envisioned
In sugar white distant dunes, devouring the modernistic
Skyscraper glass structure to a deflating tyre puncture

LIMP ECHO

A limo echo cries out in the boyish weeping lisp
The never ending darkness silently falls upon us
As we march with cadence for the tormented souls
Only blank shades filtered in through the window

Bitterly loathing from what was once chivalrous
Horrid thoughts permeate the encroaching breath
Beckoning 'bemoaning our abrupt permanent death
Insulating us from the burning coal fiery embers

Rampantly flaming out of control 'violently streaming
Across the worrying fields in our pithy menacing lives
Flickering with a canopy of stealth and eternal hatred
Stupifying the blackmailing ghastly sacrilegious abuse

We're all affectionally praying in solidarity to save the day
Bowing down in some miraculous melee; exhaustedly diminishing
Those exonerating soothing remedies, much needed to free us from
Our tormentors vice like grip where sadness always seems to drip

LIQUEFIED NUMBNESS

Are we still tripping over our tired blistered feet?
Our differences are what make us individually unique
We're detonating our angst like a rampaging sherman tank
Rummaging over leftover pieces, of the submersible crank

Contentiously conniving in a smoothily shallow watery bank
Admirably descending into the amortized liquefied numbness
Indefinitely ascribed to you're competent commodities whilst
Pivoting cautiously past the seacliffs treading on sandstone

Walls, winching upwards from this slippery fusty cliff
Tenderly tending to my jaggedly broken, bruising bones
You're life is so frustratingly thwart, like a punch drunk
Sailor, whose in dire need of a brand new exquisite tailor

LONGING ANTICIPATION

Stirring untouchable memories of unspoken thoughts an deeds
While swimming in shallow marshy swamps full of slimy reeds
My longing anticipation becomes more than some preoccupation
Darkness lurks around every corner and I'm the happy mourner

Jostling through the inequities of our evolving tangled lives
The translucent affairs stagger boldly into sequestered dives
Cauldroned in abysmal romantic attire 'delicious confections
We need to carefully conjecture all of our close transactions

MELANCHOLIC FRUSTRATION

Your like a puppet master pulling all the strings
I'm the rag doll, silently clutching at the seams
You're extracting the colour out of my imagination
Causing me to experience a melancholic frustration

As the greenhouse asphyxiates, the evergreen forests
My soul is choking relentlessly without any florists
My heart lies anchored firmly and is waiting for the next
Cooling wave to rapidly carry it out to the open blue sea

Carefully abbreviating in the chill of our delicate love
Postulating in a hastily improvised defense, in order to
Strategically immolate ourselves so we can score another chance
Just like a knight in shining armour, I thrust forward my lance

MELODRAMATIC FLUFFINESS

There's a dense film of deadly smoke permeating in the air
Blocking out the sunny sky with a pandemonium battle angst
Is there a tradition of barbarity in this soulless diligence?
It's not a one size fits all policy only a monotonous fluency

Belatedly backed an frustratingly incompetent is the yawning gap
&ou're mustachioed mouth and crinkling sore reddish eyes detest
Any forms of flattery or jitterbugging on silly conversational topics
What melodramatic fluffiness do you implore, to rise above this flaw?

MERCILESSLY STIFLE

I'm softly juggling my incapacitated emotions in
Your lava spewing pit, as you mercilessly stifle
Yourself past the intromitting superfluous traffic
Beneath this turbulent alien bombardment lies some

Very tentative approach, sparking fears of a
Koo de tah! Embezzling ourselves in raunchy dozy
Swashbuckling love; we're like bloodthirsty pirates
You n'me, roaming the endless sea trying to be free

Fiercely fighting and marauding then squishingly hoarding
The valued treasures from near 'far distant exotic lands
There's a problem that's yet to be created. Am I the cure
That's hotly debated? Is our situation dead and cremated?

MIMMICKING STANCE

The misty vapours seep into your winterchilled lips
Achingly harkening from a chockingly scented wimple
Tightening your neck, wildly you bellyflop yourself
Into a musically inclined luminously rhythmic dance

Are you saddened with love? When you take the chance
Snoozingly embracing the shakingly mimicking stance
Signalling a luscious darkness an soft burning flame
You're melancoly stormtight alibi causes me to blame

MIXING POISON

Your trying to sing, a classic song
But you can only recite first verse
The ravages of war, are so perverse
Indistinctly rationalizing a course

Your prudently whispering words of hatred
whilst miling over, a freshly dead corpse
with it's hot blood dripping in the gutter
where is you're machette sharp bone cutter

Why are you still mixing poison in my drink
Maybe your experimenting in the kitchen sink
Pre existing in a confusing realm of wonderment
My heart can no longer be consoled by tournament

MOANING INTOLERANCE

There's a seedy raft of so uncontrollable contemplation
Sentimentally aspirating in void unrestrained silliness
stifling you're spoils of the hard earned economic cash
Lunching on olive soaked calamari an dried almond patas

A distinct note of moaning intolerance sorrowfully echoes
Throughout this medieval stony dilapidated haunted castle
The stalky architecture an gothic ceilings with cathedral
Style oak beams encapsulate strange clammy spooky stories

You're befriending startled nymphs, and unfriendly ghosts
Offer the insightful curiosities allowing you to navigate
Past these menacing spasms steering yourself through many
Diplomatic impasses; to enterprising intellectual freedom

Which form of vanity do you use? To stave off this insanity
When shrewdly correcting bad habits before the light of day
What act can you seriously play? In this everchanging foray
The preliminary report suggests some covert sneaky foreplay

MYSTERIOUS DELICACIES

Your always showering me with positive energy
And tons of fun, that's why I keep on smiling
Like the Sun! I simply adore the colours from
Your turtle neck blouse n'dog jaw savvy skirt

Coupled with your silky black fishnet stockings
You're violet Caribbean drop dead skintight bra
Needs no locking; so let's put another dry log onto
The radiantly orange warm, cosy chirpy singing fire

As we drink our merlot wine n'cogly sip French champagne
Let's enjoy the steamy passion that lifts us even higher
In the midst of the foqgy night air you can reveal the mysterious
Delicacies in your shack before I launch my vile lone wolf attack

MYSTICAL AND MAGICAL

Mystical and magical you gladly ran to me
And swept my face with your fresh breeze
Clouding my eyes in you're naked stream
Appearing so bright by being too green

Mystical and magical you shone upon me
Cleansing my soul with sparkling delight
Rejoicing my mind so swiftly an bright
Causing me to suddenly faint for a while

Then renewing my upkeep exuberant style
Preening amiably and happily worthwhile
In a web of anger you abruptly ended it all
The beginning of, our majestic eternal ball

NOMADIC STALLION

I can feel your sorrow spitting down
Angrily from you're steamy sore eyes
Your ghastly altered consciousness runs
Deeply saturated with a sulking despise

Hurriedly I plead with you to curb
You're violent streak, as you seek to
Harm anyone with a protruding beak
I can sense the anger and frustration

Menacingly emanating within yourself as
I desperately try to capture your angst
Then turn it into something worthwhile
'positive for all of the world to see

An you need a trip to the local artisanal
Workshop to produce something good for me
You're like the untameable nomadic stallion
Endlessly running, whilst aiming to be free

ORAL MONTAGE

You punctured my pithy windpipe, with your
Cold heavy stare, 'ruptured my heart with
The sordid feisty lies which boldly reflect
Habitually allaying fears that we all share

Instinctually analyzing my venerating optimistic streak
Weighing up the sum recommendations that have been made
Whilst structuring the unprecedented foreign uncanny randomness
Into a significant historic project; of successive oral montage

PECULIAR COMMOTION

Emotions are wisping over orangy waters
Of the icicle infested, mingy lazy lake
I don't know how long our love will last
But wishing to be with you, is all I ask

Hastily brimming behind, the towering inferno
Intermingling in haplessly peculiar commotion
You're mind is like a winze, connecting the psyche
To another alike so let's not both get into strife

You fancied yourself, incapable of vulgarities
And you've always donated to various charities
Your analytical commentary is impudently brief
The frosty windchill, lies skimming at my teeth

PEJORATIVELY CASTIGATED

There are many discarded reminders with contrarian views
Skunking away an scampering without any logical emphasis
The harridan needs no more nurturing; dangling in excess
Baggage, hurriedly running through amber changing lights

You're questionable frozen face is a blessing in disguise
Flexible diplomacy exemplifies the adaptable jaunty prize
What observable reality is holding you so drubbingly back
Your floppy feather brown hat is convertibly hard stacked

Disbursing hazardous impediments from the long narrow track
Uninvited love lies unrelinquishly devoted next to your lap
The smutty expletives are still trumpeting through the grapevine gap
Exposing the scuttlebut babbling gossip and intoxicatantly whiffting

On charcoaled smokiness, darkening into mind rifting numbness
Treacherously spreading it's disease like the unhindered bees
Pejoratively castigated in a gurgling reticent impenetrable gird
Venturing thru unpredictably rugged arete terrain, in gear third

PERPETUALLY DISTURBED

You seem perpetually disturbed
An so parsimoniously perturbed
There's an ever puzzling hypothesis
In the midst of all the atrocities

Imbibed in a non radical prolific trance
There's no estrangement or second chance
Only an explosion of ideas in your brain
We must hurry up to catch the last train
I've seen you sleeping in the warming morning light

I know your dreaming of a love that's sweetly right
So why continue to dream? If I'm not there at night
There's a lovely subtle whisper, inside your plight

PLEASANT DREAM

I'm skipping over the rocks, beneath the bridge
Playfully chasing the squirrels up on the ridge
Running alongside the hilly embankment towards
The encapsulatingly mesmerizing, hidden valley

Emasculating your sense of worth in a creative rebirth
The summery breeze has quickly faded into autumn tease
Swimming next to the quacking ducks in the slushy lake
when I think of your gracious love, I shiver and shake

Your enthusiasm is nice. If you can dance on the pole
Refreshingly motivating yourself into a metallic role
I'll squeeze you so tightly, when you start to scream
I'll be the hero in you're deliciously pleasant dream

PONDERABLE STORIES

There are fundamental questions that we could ask
Before nodding off to a calmingly simplistic task
Where all of the whirly whispers can musically chime
Rollicking distinctly in the sync of measurable time

Slurrily I'm traipsing to a magnetic monotone vibe
Wobbling eerily in n'out of the tudor style stride
Calibrating the intriguingly bizzare puzzling evidence
Whilst contemplating the perplexing ponderable stories

Twisting within unique ideologies and powerful glories
Do you possess the inherent courage to uprightly stand
And extinquish all the ghastly evil from our pure land
If so, then we will obey you're each and every command

QUARANTINING YOU INSANE

Proceeding discreetly ill like slippery suds, your life
Is like a supernova, fizzing out in a short lived blaze
Provisioning for the doom an gloom off setting scenario
This allocated portfolio alienates all forms of success

Wriggling out of your sweaty shirt flashing your dry toned legs
Showing off your silky smooth hairless muscled worked out chest
You're jumping off air tight plumpy chequered coloured cushions
Then rolling over onto the 70's styled shagpile woollen carpets

Slightly disgruntled you stalk like a fat smelly agitated dog
The bittersweet recollections have fractured your morphed ego
Cunningly you despise an fervently ostracise our lovable vein
So many skeptical thoughts and ideas have crept in your brain

Undecidingly your pondering an unnerving truce which tests your game
You're cooked up, in an emotionally hellish state under lock n'chain
Nevertheless you're so restless and seek release, from all this pain
But I'll keep you circulating on a dog leash quarantining you insane

RAMPANT PROFANITY

I'll cross over the narrow bridges of insanity
With a substantial amount of rampant profanity
To reach the threshold of your inner sanctum
The angels still call your sweet chummy name

As the heavens playfully reconnect your glorious aim
Attentively watching over your sore mischievous game
Beckoning with lustful sensuality your solemn virtue
And chastity have been battered and culpably damaged

Dressed in brightly soiled linen and loin cloth garments
Your subtle hints an intentions aren't purely honourable
Hatching a votive image, like a septuagenarian pensioner
Here comes a grey bearded man trying to offload his plan

RECEDING INNOCENCE

Looking out of the frosty window
An icy bright wilderness reveals
The unimposing presence creeping
In our dreamy receding innocence

So tantalizingly crisp is the mountain air
Above the hungry wolf's lair, exasperating
With lamented tunes and tree lopping crews
There goes an Alaskan polar, searching for

Something solar! My socks are warming in the
Cat's cradle above the fireplace's ashy dust
There's a subtle hint of pseudo intellectual
Connotations mixed in old wives explanations

REFLECTIVELY BACKPEDDLING

You're gouging eyes are inductive to the burdened
Corrugations; premised in your crater soiled face
The developed catchworks are notoriously accentuated
By superlative alternatives with puffable expletives

That are ingrained in your robust bittersweet psyche
Reflectively backpeddling, in an inequitable society
You're intimate concentration is capable of propriety
Those irreparable damages, keep reducing your variety

REFRESHING AMBIENCE

As the cooling calm river's water gradually flow
Will you let you're laughter affectionately grow
Then we can put on a pleasing jubilant funny show
You're sigh is like an eclipse shining with a bow

I am trapped in bleak conformity trying to break free
There are insulative properties randomly clutching me
Like photooxidation scooping with systemic penetration
Sunshine rays filter thru stained glass church windows

Reflecting a sombrous fairytale refreshing ambience
We've been mustered like sailors at the ships rails
As we keep desperately banging upon the rusty nails
Shall we recapitulate our lives before we set sails

RETRACE OUR FOOTSTEPS

How can you wear a coat without any pockets
Or a business type shirt without no buttons
We can retrace our footsteps 'rekindle ourselves
Especially when we're towing, those angelic bells

You're motion is whirling like a downgraded
Tropical cyclone, there's a virtual reality
Desperately trying to find a safe haven abode
But they always keep changing the secret code

Just imagine if a blind man could suddenly see
Then he would wake up from his miserable dream
He'd surely scream loudly with a phonetic glee
The miracles of modern science have blessed me

He would become the centrepieceof his block
The neighbours will curiously jitterbug talk
We have to live our lives with some reality and hope
Because the future depends on how we're able to cope

RETREATING CHILL

Dark scolding clouds bring cool droplets
Of rain in a long awaited summery shower
Crispy vapours rise up in steamy forests
Gently staining my sweaty blistery palms

Like a gleaming embrace rubbing your chest
Next to mine. I know someday we'll be fine
There's a retreating chill up my spine, as
Our spirited prancing feet mockingly stray

Roaming up the treacherously windswept cliff
With glazing eyes and a thirsty hungry mouth
Tethering in a dark crimson waxing full moon
Dreaming of amorous tales of love quite soon

REVIVIFIED STATE

Sitting like sentiment at the bottom of the shallow pond
Dazzlingly extricating yourself from the pressing issues
There's the massive hole in you're rapidly deteriorating life
You seek a governor's pardon but that's just plausible jargon

Deleteriously drenched; your wallowing in a godless state
Absurdly yelping, sparsely imploding in a revivified leap
Through the rusting farmqate we run up the floating steps
To an elevated hilly grassy lawn, beyond the pencil pined

Trees, we sit amongst the illiterate cow faced chatting locals
Momentarily observing they're floaty layers of simple elegance
Affordably been washed away into the garbage bin of wasted
    history
Instead of sitting in the shade refurbished dwellings offer relief

Instilled in the roots of fear, we need to drastically overhaul
Ourselves; and redecorate to a rationale that's logically clear
Restoring orderliness in regular context, is aesthetically late
Soothing the oppressive weight by a sacerdotal revivified state

SCARS OF STRIFE

The windblown grass is littered with sad stories of
Shipwrecked ghost ships 'abandoned old rusty boats
Rotting away at the seams just like my tortured life
Has recklessly been; as I venture down that freezing

Breezy rainy road I'm getting soaked but wizened with
All the things I see. Your courting style fetters the
Lovelight which you have shone shaping any prexisting views
You're degradedly lustful; yet tranquilly humble and serene

Like the windy trill that ruffles in the greyish skies
Withering leaves never grieves swirving by the wayside
I've debunked your beliefs, in idiotic conspiracy theories
N'hastily too often thought off nonsical dried up querries

Without real hard edged scientific evidence, and skeptical inquiries
We try to avoid the inevitable collision course of factual rivalries
There exists scars of strife behind the tightly shut mucky gate
    door
That keeps on eerily swinging 'craving for us to enter it once
    more

SCREECHING SORE EYES

If I had to lie
If I had to sigh
Would you always be with
Me, in verse and stride?

You can't fib at me or
Look at me in the eye
So you tell me a quick
Postgraduate subtle lie

Why demoralize and ostracize with screeching sore eyes
You should find another hobby to glamorize n'harmonize
An don't hide behind a mirriod of false deceitful lies
Which add up to nothing more than vain fruitless cries

Now let's make it abundantly clear
Before you and me vanish with fear
We shall rekindle our loving scenario
Then celebrate our wedding in Ontario

SCRUPULOUS FRIGIDITY

Your prancing around like a bold heroic figure
From some depressively sadistic neolithic myth
But you're really dancing barefooted in 3/4 time
To the sounds of the electronic moog synthesizer

Stoically holding your head so sparkling high
Because in the next chapter you'll be trashed
Then die! When you lock your hips onto mine
And hold me tenderly close I can freely fly

I feel like I'm walking on the river's water
As if I'm your long lost inebriated daughter
Your solidly occupying patches of dirt which
You hope will turn into gold before your old

Where's the validity for the scrupulous frigidity
There's no pretence, for the nail biting suspense
You have to cross the line to finish the race
But you keep on stumbling flat on you're face

SECULAR FRATERNITY

You're deliriously twisted psyche keeps on morphing
Into delectable nuances, streamed with complexities
Partially submerging strange thoughts in a plethora
Of infringing frantic agenda, backlogged into a non

Secular fraternity: we're narrowly grappling to
Achieve a comprehensive synopsis as part of our
Purification program; like a castle under siege
Our addictive love catapults my heart with ease

As polar ice caps reflect heat from the sun to the land
The temptation of having you with me is awkwardly grand
Do we worship our world leaders, for their leadership alone?
How many of us do really wish to discreetly bring them home?

SEQUESTED GLORY

You're reliving a moment from the sequested glory
Frolicking at your illustrious, pivotal ascension
You've been left abandoned by the unforgiving mad
Armies which you eagerly volunteered to fight for

Your advanced witticism 'outlandish remarks leave
You alone in the ditch dark; drying up you're bone
Thin pale face, it's such a remorseful sorrowful case
The excessive trivialities proved to be hurtfully sad

Condemning yourself to a bemoaning delusional state
Crammed into a plethora, of pent up volcanized hate
Maligning fervidly with swollen heavy tears and hidden fears
Can you vanquish all the hurt instilled throughout the years

SHIBBOLETH

I'm zealously trying to decode you're
Shibboleth continuum abstract message
That has got me so terribly bogged down
I'm showing my blob faced wrinkly lines

The frustration, keeps mustering higher
My deflating legs feel like a flat tyre
A sharp object must have punctured them
An left me confounded burning like fire

Your mind is just a blank, soiled canvass sheet
Calling upon imagination to draw a cartoon neat
Is there a conspiracy emerging beneath our feet
What has been hushed up repelled and now delete

You've been tossed 'tussled in the migrating sea
You look like a shipwrecked sailor, all washed up
On some unknown unchattered salty sandy shores
Can you find any relief, in the amoebic pores?

SMUGGLING FEARS

I shudder to think, about the rapid velocity
Which your ego exploded and randomly thudded
Then our world scudded into a venomous shift
The bearings that support the turning shafts

Have all but rustily withered away, your rafts
Keep voyaging steadily as the friction affrays
Like the smuggling fears which we constantly allay
We're all sentenced to death! But we wish to delay

STALEMATE CALAMITY

I feel like we're trespassing on forgotten ancient soil
Isn't this land sacred to the ones who fought with toil
Transforming your begotten mindset, in a secondary coil
I'm a die hard lover of liberty so I'll break the curse

And pursue freedom by replenishing your soul from the hungry
Thirst; inducing a nightshade of meritoriously meshing mirth
Sterilizing the silver coated instruments to deflect any flaws
Thus examining any symbols of purity, extracted from the tardy

Concentrated primeval furceps, dipped in aluminium tips
Swooping 'stripping away the lust from your weary eyes
Whilst theatrically performing the continuous syncopated ragtime
Melody, complicated in a less than impressive stalemate calamity

STERILE REJECTIONS

When you shed away that saucy icy cold bitter stare
You'll know that you have someone to genuinely care
Do you believe in extraterrestrial beings from other planets
Or gigantic squids that inhabit the murky bottomless fathoms

We could bypass the stenosis of strange affections
And the heartless forms of post sterile rejections
Your temper is boiling like a hot steamy kettle
Thus I'm feeling flustered and rather unsettled

One illusion leads to another, spilling over into milieu
Sordid senseless clutter; there's some artless absurdity
Of incomprehensible delusion, ticking off with profusion
we should all try to obtain the proper relevant infusion

SUBTRACTIVELY RECRUNCHING

There's a merging of philosophies an clever ideas
Exclusively untouchable in theory and in practice
They claim to be the answer. But no theory realistically
Contains the entire answer! By subtractively recrunching

The hard earned additives of our many attainable goals
What was once a scarcity, is now in complete abundance
With an artistic flick of the wrist we can get the gist
There are endless sheer delights as we leisurely stroll

Perpendicularly by the crystal clear shallow sleepy river
I'm so enthralled with your lengthy, caramelised hot kiss
That I'm reduced to blushing hushed tears every time we meet
Your adventurous spirit always puts you in the driver's seat

SUBMISSIVE LIE

You're like a caged up bird
Furiously flapping it's wings
Desperately trying to break free
It's a dauntless task. Don't you agree?

Transpiring in a new resource
Generating wildly off course
The wind is whistling in your sails
Golden sands are left in your trails

The protocol of the fox is sabre sly
Even if we use the illuminati eye
Can we win without an incumbent try
How can we spruik our submissive lie

SUCK THE MARROW

Your like a frail inconspicious insect
Been swept away by the storming waters
Into the dirty toxic slimy muddy creek
Your attempting to suck the marrow out

Of the bone, but you're heart is set in stone
Are you sneakingly dropping your smelly shoes
Off your callous feet? That's not really neat
Then you miserly stroll around like the noble

Kingfisher bird with it's glossy blue green back
Your semi conscious as you grubbily sleep in the
Jute cloth sack; you love astronomy 'embrace the
Free trade economy, your mathematically smart and

Brave in heart! But you're no scientific genius, so
The words you often speak are seldom short of grief
There are many rivers and canals that you can cross
But you still fall well short of being the big boss

SWAMPY BAYOU

You're unsympathetic smile paints a disturbing picture
In my mind, your like a prairie dog chasing cottontail
Rabbits. up the soggy marshy ferny steep climbing hills
Running through puffing smoke of bush hiker's campfires

Dressed in polka dotted fur lined jackets, we clumsily
Jumped onto the awaiting steam driven ferryboats as to
Reach safer shores, refusing to take command of oneself
Yet resuming orders on board the relaxing cruise liners

Leading into a secure fogbound coast your brittly dyed
Purplish hair resembles oyster grass rhizone sediments
Being flushed from the murky swampy bayou alligator wetlands
Proselytizing in a fringe of sooty soil covered in dirty oil

TAKEOVER ALIGNMENT

Sparks are flashing from your bruised jittery knuckles
As you're up to your armpits in thick stinky slimy mud
There's an intoxicating waft of densely charcoaled vapours
As you callously acquaint yourself with strange bedfellows

A sudden dose of silliness has compounded into a sad melee
Uncalled for rumblings are unfurlingly jiggling n'writhing
Lovingly embracing yourself in a shallow thoughtless conversation
An uncharacteristic display of affection needs delicate attention

The fluffiest of flowers keep blightedly bubbling like rapidly
Disappearing seashell deposits sinking in solitary confinement
You do look auspiciously cute in theatrically wearable costumes
Dredging up the superficial uncertainty in a takeover alignment

TENANTS ON THIS PLANET

You don't want to be a prisoner of the old past
Buried in the shackles of conformist mediocrity
But you seek to be a pioneer of the near future
So you can precisely nurture whatever suits you

Are you eagerly awaiting, in tense anticipation
For long overdue self esteem orderly citation
I desperately try to sail on the cool calm seas
But I'm plunged into casks of a worrying breeze

This unfortunate episode is tepidly disintergrating
Into a hyper ventilating, paranoid form of euphoria
You've been confined to your covetous cinema shaped
Two bedroom apartment, overlooking the fire station

Transcending a bygone, productive revolutionary era
Leaving behind a besettling avant garde copper hued
Liturgy; sugarcoating the sparkling tin shack gables
Adjacent to neighbouring streets and demolishing the

High pitched sultry toppy vibrantly ringing belltower
As well as my craftily put together curative gestures
I feel like we're tenants on this planet; just serving time
Perhaps future generations can gasp at what we leave behind

TICKLING MY RIBS

If you keep telling me how
Sweet I am, I'll turn into
Honey; the sweetness will drip
Emblazoningly on my red cheeks

Till everything's sunny; so try
Telling me fibs and tickling my
Ribs ! I want to gradually go to
where no one has gone before an

Knock upon Heaven's door, if I'm
Accepted I'll give a lion's roar
You know how hard I'll try to always
Satisfy! especially when I'm so high

I'll stay off the booze till I'm dry
An you can quietly drive by as I cry
Then I'll live another memorable day
Before I've withered away with decay

TRITURATING MECHANISM

I'm braving all the emotions you omit
To have you I know that I must submit
My entire life for you I'll gladly commit
Not even a fraction of care, shall I omit
We'll stick together, just like siamese twins
And throw away all of the rubbish in the bins
I'll keep broadcasting my love thru the debris
Of human desperation nullifying a disenchanted

Contracting heart that franchises you're creation
In psychology there's elaborate terminology, even
Beyond the compound of safe haven; into the sucking
Triturating mechanism devoid of any colourful prism

UNBEKNOWINGLY DISTURBED

I'm swimming out off the well of qrief
And running into the rugged wilderness
I'm confronted with endless loneliness

You're like a snarling, hungry wild lion
Constantly ramping up the pressure on me
Dissapating hope which I need to receive

The tautness in your tone has a lulling pitch
Sublimating your senses, from a teasing bitch
Perhaps there's a bad habit you wish to ditch

You're life is butchering upon a chopping block
Akin to a centuries old dusty oil burning clock
So why do you trade in your old gun for a glock

This petty bickering makes you unbeknowingly disturbed
Delicately indented is the appropriate new way to turn
There are many unnatural disasters which you seek to avoid
Those easily obtainable pleasing luxuries rekindle the joy

UNCEASINGLY TAUNT

What idioms of the heart shall you employ
How many botch potch affairs do you enjoy
What seditious demands will you readily deploy
When the pediment is about to fall on your toy

There's a concept behind the outlandish design
That's why we need to realign then we can dine
Are you still waiting for the water to stealthily rise
In order to raise your boat; sailing in the soggy moat

The turmoil comes embroided with the stretchiest imagination
Turning over some unceasingly taunt, meaningless frustration
What has happened to your once privileged irrational escapade
Has the ransom exceeded what you've already incurred and paid

UNCERTAIN OBSTACLES

The boomerang of your love is steadily flying away
Leaving my heart dithering in slithering disarray!
Your constantly jumping around like a two bob clown
Living dangerously like a hunter, tracking his prey

Baiting the wildlife victim with a cunning display
Carefully observing; like an aircraft pilot that's
Looking for an open clearing to safely land the plane
Those uncertain obstacles in life are hardly the same

Metaphysically speaking; they're calling you're name
Skepticism and logic keep battling us with vain pain
Accumulating wisdom an discipline are offered to a select
Reserved few, the rest of society lacks the faintest clue

UNEARTHLY KINGS

You're unorthodox trisagion hymns
Pay homage to the unearthly kings
With unison passion everyone sings
Rare holy qifts the faithful bring

Deplorably trite, are the speculative defences
Lamely wheedling out all of the fake pretences
So why do you still take your problems to bed?
You know you'll sleep better when you're dead!

I have travelled to places where no one else has
Ever been; digging through mines of minerals and
Valleys of green, suppressing revolts from angry peasants
Paupers n'queen, keeping the revolution alive in my dream

UNHEALED SCARS

Can you hear the angry muffled murmur
In the distance of the tinkling bells
Our love shines brightly like sparkling wells
The dust keeps rising on pale gravelled roads

Clattering cries playfully creep to rattle your soul
The chimney chocked as our time was suddenly revoked
Shrieking in a blotched legacy of soulless desires
Unhealed scars are burning like scolding bushfires

Waves are crashing as our ego's are intolerably clashing
This selflessly martyred aloneness drifts past our lives
A disabled man needs to hurriedly find a comfortable seat
Whilst motherless starving children still cry at our feet

UNIMPEDEDLY PROMENADING

Unimpededly promenading to uncoupling the intruding pains
Your submerged in stiffness towards a very ignoble degree
Listening to murmuring conversations; all fakeness has been
Revealed! Reconnoitering your status by furthering yourself

There's a rampant recrimination dishevelling mixed intergration
And your stomach is grumbling loudly for some finger food
    lunch
I do remind you that we're more than just a boastful lazy bunch
Tizziedly spawned; you stutter with a demonstrably slyish
    hunch

As you carefully point then squirt you're foul mouthed venom
Like a desert rattler curling amongst the fiery barren rocks
Quickly hiding yourself into the burning hot wavy powdery
    sand
You're treacherous fangs are so brutally sharp yet nimbly pang

UNWITTINGLY CARES

We're needlessly dumping urges in our abstract minds
Wishing to hear the rustling of the shady palm trees
Desperately trying to grasp the last drop of sunlight
In the shaded calmness of the lazy cool autumn breeze

Then I ran inside to light the iconic church candles
To say my prayers to God above who unwittingly cares
Our son is now the proud captain of an aircraft ship
who is usually concerned of passenger safety on trip

VACUUM OF NOTHINGNESS

Your like a white gloved cute little bellboy
Who's anxiously waiting to collect a big tip
Clinging onto the edge of your worn out seat
Hanging on every line that the actor's speak

Brilliance occurs in so many unexpected variable ways
Strangely criticising the divisively predominant days
So why keep wending over sundry camouflaged carnage
Surely, you can conjobble much more serious mileage

I'm cordially licking my lips then clenching my fists
As the memory of our love drives me insane.
I'm still whining from the pain, frantically soul searching in a
Vacuum of nothingness; willing to serve an not perturb

VERITABLE CHOICES

It's a pressure cooker situation where you can
Change you're destiny with a stirring vexation
Once subjected to a campaign of Ireful bigotry
You've reached boiling point, then fought back

Within a satirizing disobedience you've organized
A revolution, and demonstrated a new constitution
The combined forces have admonished all resources
We've managed to eliminate; the veritable choices

VEXING ATTITUDES

Leadership is all about connecting with
Inspiration and collaboration, spanding
The creatively new productive formation
So let's avoid the inescapable scenario

There's a collision of vexing attitudes and
Troubling experiences; garishly pecking out
Some necessary momentum needed to muster the
Appropriate outcome. It's akin to a tea bag!

You won't know how it will taste like
Till you put it in a cup of hot water
Ungraciously you can never do what you ought to
You just jerk around like a rebellious daughter

VULGARIAN SUBORDINATION

You're sparsely living like a scavenger gatherer
Remaining isolated from the outside modern world
And fleeing further than most people have ever dared
Saturating the precious stocks 'bonds; as you cared

You're lustful green eyes twinkle so adorably abrupt
You're just like a treacherous, marauding hungry fox
Wading viciously from town to town in the dark night
The ominous vulgarian subordination is not yet right

WADDLING WONDOROUSLY

You're prying eyes are watching over the
Glacial floes an cheery bubbling streams
Which are so beauteously rich and serene
With prideful insecurity the remnants of

Yesteryear need enduring commitment distinctively quick
We're waddling wondrously beyond the revolving circles
Categorically elutriating from the synchronous shift
Precociously fueling the strumming strings as a gift

WHISPERING LULLABIES

Flowing juices of untapped angel zephyr springs
Ambigiously scrolled by ancient prophetic kings
Your fierce pride acknowledges the fear you hide
Scattered visions snatch the chimes as you glide

The harmonies keep wafting over my delicate lies
Peering inquisitively, with your perceptive eyes
I can hear the reioicing of whispering lullabies
Waving goodbye from the moment when you were sly